Acknowledgement of Country

I acknowledge the Traditional Custodians of the land on which this work was written and created, the Turrbal and Yugara peoples of Meanjin, and I pay my deep respects to their Elders, past, present, and emerging.
I honour their unbroken connection to land, language, story, and culture, and recognise that sovereignty was never ceded.
I extend this respect to all First Nations peoples across Australia, whose voices, histories, and creative traditions continue to guide and enrich this place.

Dopamine of Destruction

By

M Renae Dubois

Contents

Awakened to the evil that I think
may lurk within
The attitude I hold that made me think I
didn't sin
Through my actions I've dealt cards that
have been known to knock around
The recipients, and believers that my
behaviour would be sound
No person to excuse my pain at the things
that I now know
That I harbour inner cruelty and a propensity
to go
Dark places in my fantasies what do they
actually reveal
Who is the dire figure who creates the
wicked deal?
Long ago was planted, a seed of discontent
Now I live with an unhappiness and my
anger's sometimes spent
Must accept the yin inside me but feed the
yang to grow

So the loving senses in my heart and my actions will just flow

Bones of a baby

Soft and quite ply
But they are the individuals
Ego inside
The bones of the baby
They will develop
The friction of living
The words it inhabits
The physical body is
More than two parts
Like the bones of the ego
Or the depth of the heart
To shatter a bone means
Reality collides
But it heals with some care that is
Applied from outside
So the baby's bones might seem like
They're not really there
Like the baby's just smiling
Without any care
But the visions surrounding
The baby will bloom
Soon her ego will grow
And fill up the room

Deliberate idiot

Insane she will claim
The reality hidden
The objective, a game
Twisting of ethics
Create, yet confine
The manner of living
The unique design
With vision, the future a
Wondrous goal
Of creation and music and
Art that feels whole
The language of common
Theories, ideas
The usual, the hopes, the
Depression and fears
The vision is costly, and
Different to those
But, to ask the hard questions
Her spirit will grow

Perception, an embodiment

Of arrogance and lies
The things we tell ourselves
To stay in a disguise
Rose-tinted glasses though they look
They will not see inside
This absent-minded search for life
Is actually a disguise
The people walk with fear, appear
With anxiety in their eyes
The determination to get through
Their tension undisguised
Judgement cast before a thought
They're inbuilt to divide
The elevated thought is sought
But the truth is its disguise
Where one may walk there'll always be
The one who does comply
But right within the beat of him
His heart is still disguised
To shed the skin of what we are
To realise what implies
When treating our anxiety

As its very own disguise

Theres a version of Him up there

A depiction of a form
Of both temperament and context
In what clothes shall he be worn
The image is indicative
Of the sculptor's graceful hand
The love he has for subject
The God in form of man
All the beauty he can sum up
His perception he adores
This creature of Creator
Creators creature making more

To pay the price of seeing
What others cannot bear
The insistence that they share with me
All the things for which they care
Cos I try to get them thinking
But it scares them all away
They're leaving feeling attacked and
My intellects no display
Intelligence of arrogance?
A wit or a true shit?
I lol, but that’s the heart of it,
The drama that is lit
So alone in understanding every-
Thing they cannot see
And my ego doesn't coach me
On a better way to be
So my anger is directed at
The ones who have their own
Inner missions and their wisdoms
That to me they will not loan
Too interrogative, and arrogant
Theres a lot of words I use
That are repeated very often

Because the truth is, I abuse
I get angry, I cast judgement,
I do not treat them the same way
That I feel I deserve richly and
In fact, I make them pay

I'm careful with my comforts
And my companion too
My confidential mentor
The one who holds the clue
Cos I'm carrying a care of
Contempt for casual ways
A cornerstone of company
Is conversing, what we say
Cutting corners in the words they use
Crafting cunning kinds of lies
Confusing those who cannot see
The cruelty in their eyes
The callous lack of care for how
Their charges can be kept
The constant literation that will
Kill but not forget

The colour was reminding her
Colouring her perception
The black inside the room
But golden light on her reflection
Like a bird within her nest in the
Dark light of the moon
And the clarity encompassing
When the light fits with her mood
Theres a rouge of flush there forming
As the realisations bared
The truth for which she's seeking
The very thing for which she cares
Is now within the physical
Not just in her mind
And the light that's slowly burgeoning
Leaves the night behind

The cost will not again be paid

The subject changes form
Decision made, Investment paid
A familiar tale reborn
With his temperament and secrets
That he keeps as a defence
So she gives not really knowing
Cos he’s always on the fence
Those eyes that will not look at her
They shift and move with care
The brown in them becomes a pale
Reflection of his air
Not present in his heart he keeps
His thoughts right to himself
Yet his body is a comfort and
For her some sexual health
But the cost upon her soul when he
Takes his time and more
She gives but he won't pay her price
Next morning she feels poor

A faith in human decency and
Ability to not dwell
To see the past behind you and to
Know your present well
It's not much to ask of anyone
It's what I need to know
If they're stepping in familiar tread
If we're carried by same flow
But the wishing for familiar
While some interest still remains
Is another opportunity for
Him to play his game
And like little leaves I'm damaged
By the coldness in the air
Like when I'm talking to him, and
At anything, he will stare
I'm talking to myself and I
Know the way to go
To live like I don't need someone
I can't let this bastard know
That I'm feeling very lonely and
I can't take it anymore
I worry 'bout my temperament
I don't need to lock the doors

Noones coming, they don't even
Ring, there’s no one that’s out there
And I cannot keep pretending that I
Really just don't care.

What do I need a man to be?

On what do I grade masculinity?
Is it the presence all feel when he walks in a room?
Or the need to get physical, sometimes too soon?
Does he stands like a statue and never reveal
The things that he cares for, the way that he feels?
Is it the practice of spent bodies and sweat?
Or a day of the labouring, using his head?
Does it matter if he cooks, spends quality time
With his mother he treats as loving divine?
It's the way that he notices, quietly checks
That I'm doing ok with our kids and the rest
The action of doing the chores around the house
To sit with our children, to love me, his spouse
He shows love in his actions and always feels free
To express his emotions or vulnerability

The question I find now, is how to respond?
What role can I play so his ego will hold?
The acts of the loving, are the strength and the aim
Of being, believing, and the joy will remain

Feeling pretty stranded

Like a whale upon the beach
Though the people they surround me
They can't or will not reach
They stand with silence, blame me
For the state that I am in
And they wonder very loudly
What could have done me in
While the ocean with its currents
And waves and crushing tides
Is behind me but the cause of
And reason I describe
In my songs of pain and weakness
I beseech the ones who care
But they're fearful and unsure so
They just stand with woeful stare
And my body is left to the sun
The shrinking of skin tone
My inner vision does not fit
So far from my soul's home

Solitude isn't a safe place
But everywhere that I go is the same
The unique but familiar responses
The look on their face, the disdain
Should I go out and into the stranger
Places with people who smile
But the comfort is just an illusion
I feel the fake, and hear the denials
Noone will be honest and say it
But if they did, you would feel more alone
Like the reasons are really within you
The disgustingness really your own
To climb out and to hold with an ego
Is to embrace the danger that's felt
Like to find in a fire, cotton cushion
An impossible security held

The rug was thrown aghast, aside
Scratches on these painted walls
The sounds encased in soundproof tiles
The vision hints at mission stalled
Through lavender and purple too
The vision of what she had seen
Its not just walls that rendered blue
A need to move to deem to clean
She felt the touch the rough the clutch
The memory of a sudden doom
He did it still too hard too much
And still exists in this her room

Once history has been named
And all the bad men shamed
The women will be blamed
Always is the same
In case of further view
Look past inner you
Anticipate the room
Creating your own tune
I could stay beside
This creature who has lied
From me he always hides
And always I have cried
So why bring him to your room?
His energy back so soon
He needs his manners groomed
You need to just assume
That things will stay the same
That he just won't be tamed
And soon your heart is slain
And again, you will be blamed

May I have lived too long to be afraid
To stand in tears my feelings frayed
I conquer some but still fall short
Let no one free from pain, I hurt
It won't be long I know the day
Until the entirety away
Then I can leave and grieve and see
The universe cold it is to me

It’s funny how intensity
Rivals the relevancy
The spoken word's acidity
Destroys an amiability
And friendships hang - fragility

She knows she has ability
To see the real complexity
And marvel at the absurdity
She speaks with an authority
More confident, she'll try to be

She's building her capacity
Not compatibility
She needs to feel security
She'll write in perpetuity
Her words, her thoughts, her musicality

Somewhat overwhelming when the vision is at hand
When the pen has hit the paper and I don't know how it lands
The collection of the many ways the light has grown within
But the wisdom to know otherwise just where it has gone dim
Putting pen to paper acts upon the feelings in the soul
It clarifies reality, helps to see it whole
The gathering of memories and the sage advice they give
Widens and illuminates the way in which to live

The dawn of understanding

Though the vision was impaired
The crystallising morning
When the girl was more aware
Sight now shed of prior meaning
Colours coming through the clouds
All the fogged interpretation
Of her past, what was allowed
Though the ground is not quite visible
There are no guiding paths
She recognises meaning
And feels joy within her heart
With a breath she sends it flying
All the clouds and rules before
And she welcomes all the visions
All the hopes she has in store

Within my hands the argument to me is pliable and felt
Like clay upon the potter's wheel, but one that will be dealt
I have it in my fingers that will rationalise my form
But my mother's turn is coming and with fear my heart is torn
With another I might share the shaping, see the things they must
Like a conversation happening, just relinquish and then trust
That the clay will not be watered down with platitudes of care
Or wiped off the equipment, told to clean it, how I dare!
I've been sitting at this potter's wheel, alone and in the dark
And the closest I can get to understanding is a fuck

Epilogue

To think of craving meaning in the entire universe
Doesn’t seem like that is needed or a part of what is called Absurd
When Kafka and our Camus wrote of men within the grip
Of a state of mind that meant that they were heading for the clink
I don't perceive a desperate push for them to make some sense
They carry on their daily tasks, with duty that’s intense
The mission for Meurcault was to get out of the sun
And Kafka’s charactcr didn’t ask why he was the one
No, their attitude was very sure but not with any depth
Or at least they couldn't see the very structures in their heads
They persisted in the shallow skin that life was displaying
And the meaning if there was one, was these two men in their greying

Its impossible to consider them as light, no they are intense
Intent on sticking to what to them will make some sense
I guess these characters are meant to show and demonstrate
That depending on a structure means you're left to others fate

The absurd is not mentality, or personal trait or quality
It's the way the world has to be, with civilisation, society
The effort to achieve a goal, to know the truth, embrace your soul
It does not fit that you will know. The point is nil, the meaning low
You may be shocked to realise the depths and lengths of others lies
You may decide in your own eyes to never run or try disguise
The structures you exist within, like running just to place in bin
You once were told that you had sinned, now you look further in
Absurdity is going to seem, a kind of hallucinogenic dream
But you will find that it is clean of what's predicted and what it means

Ideas

Camus' absurd is vertical, one man to the cosmos. My definition is that absurdity is societal (horizontal), with many conflicting present meanings, beliefs, ways and whys of searching. Everybody starts somewhere, whether it be in a beautiful furnished home or in the worst of circumstances. We all start with an understanding, we all come from somewhere, which makes the societal landscape even more convoluted and absurd, in its entirety.

About the Author

M Renae Dubois is a Brisbane poet, painter, and student of Philosophy. Since suffering a head injury at the age of 16 in the early 90s, Renae has written with graduating technical skill and with emerging original philosophical insights, starting from her earliest perceptions after her head injury. She lives peacefully, enjoying personal study, reading, and the company of her friends and family.

Head Injury Pros and Cons *(Originally published as Curses of Verses: A Head Injury Tale 2020 by XLibris) 24 Dec, 2025*

Utterly : A Biography in Verse *(First published in 2023 by Clark & Mackay) 22 Jan, 2026*

Coy Candour *2025*

Crosschairs *7 Feb, 2026*

Curses of Verses: A Composite *(Books 1-3 plus epilogue) 8 March 2026*

An Encounter : Poetry, Existentialism *9 May, 2026*

Wreck : A Reckoning *1 Jun, 2026*

Percevity *28 Jun, 2026*

BPD : A Memoir – Beyond Personal Destruction *(penned 2004) 30 Jun, 2026*

Dopamine of Destruction *27 Aug, 2026*

www.cursesofverses.com

www.ingramcontent.com/pod-product-compliance
Lightning Source LLC
LaVergne TN
LVHW050751061126
851857LV00013B/1099
* 9 7 8 1 7 6 4 9 2 4 8 1 8 *